Farm Animals

Farming is the most important occupation in the world. Nearly all the food we eat comes from crops and livestock raised on farms. In the past, the typical American family of the 1700s and 1800s barely raised enough food for themselves. The family raised cattle, chickens, and hogs and grew crops and vegetables. Horses plowed the fields. Since then, scientific advances have made farming increasingly specialized and productive. Today each farmer produces enough food to feed 80 people. Farming has become an important business run by large corporations and is no longer a way of life as it was in the past. Today, smaller private farms provide food diversity and availability.

Across

3. This strong animal, once used to pull a plow, is now raised mainly for riding.

4. The female bovine is most often raised on a dairy farm.

5. Most of these animals are raised for meat on hog farms.

7. This animal has provided people with milk, meat, and wool since prehistoric times.

9. A domestic one is raised for its meat and fur, for use in scientific research, and as a pet.

Down

1. These are among the most important animals in the world because they provide both food and clothing.

2. Raising this animal for meat and eggs is a major industry.

6. This waterbird is raised for its meat and for its down (soft feathers).

8. We think of this animal as part of a traditional Thanksgiving and Christmas dinner.

chicken
cow
goat
goose
horse
pigs
rabbit
sheep
turkey

1

Homographs

Some words have more than one meaning. There are two clues for each word in the puzzle. Think of a word that fits both clues. Write the word in the puzzle.

Across

4. not heavy
   to set on fire

5. to conveniently arrange papers
   a tool with ridges used to smooth surfaces

7. a unit of weight equal to 16 ounces
   to hit with a heavy blow

8. a big dance
   a round object used in sports

Down

1. a warning sound made by a kind of snake
   a baby's toy that makes noise when shaken

2. an herb, tree, or shrub
   to put in the ground so that it will grow

3. friendly, generous
   sort or variety

6. part of the body at the end of the arm
   to pass or give something to someone

7. to have fun
   a story that is acted out on a stage

ball
file
hand
kind
light
plant
play
pound
rattle

2

Trucks

Trucking is a major industry in the United States. Trucks carry food to grocery stores, gasoline to service stations, manufactured goods from factories to stores; nearly everything we eat, drink, wear, and use has been delivered by truck. Trucks vary greatly in size. Most trucks have more powerful engines than automobiles and are built for rugged work. Manufacturers produce many of kinds of trucks. They are classified into three main groups: light, medium, and heavy. The groups are based on gross vehicle weight, the combined weight of the truck and the load it carries.

Across

1. a popular, light-duty truck with an open bed

2. carries liquids such as milk, oil, or gasoline

4. a large, roomy, medium truck used for moving furniture or other bulky items

5. works at construction sites to unload material as the rear of the truck tilts the contents

7. mixes and pours a strong material that has many uses such as the foundation of buildings

Down

1. an all-purpose flatbed truck with rails, often used on farms

3. comes to our homes and businesses to collect refuse

6. a light truck popular with small businesses such as floral shops for delivering their goods

concrete
dump
garbage
panel
pickup
platform
tank
van

Nursery Rhymes

Nursery rhymes have been passed on verbally for centuries. Every culture has its own nursery rhymes plus additional ones that have been adopted from other countries. There are many origins for the rhymes. Ballads, prayers, proverbs, tavern songs, and fragments of ballads account for many of the rhymes. A nursery rhyme is a rhythmical poem that amuses or soothes young children. Many pass on cultural information and values and help children appreciate the sounds and rhythms of a language.

Cow
Humpty Dumpty
Jack
Jack and Jill
Little Bo Peep
London
Mary
Mouse
Old Woman
Peter
Spider
Three

Across

1. what ran up the clock
4. who went up the hill
6. who lived in a shoe
7. who was a pumpkin eater
8. what jumped over the moon
10. who lost her sheep
11. who had a little lamb

Down

2. what went up a water spout
3. who fell off a wall
4. who jumped over a candle stick
5. what bridge is falling down
9. how many men were in a tub

5

Travel

Across

5. bring in case it rains

6. small note, usually with a photograph on one side, sent by mail

9. a day assigned by the government to honor a person, event, or idea

10. a place to swim

11. a vehicle that travels on roads

12. a vehicle that travels in the sky

14. a person visiting a place from out of town

15. an object in which clothes and other items are packed

Down

1. a place for pets to stay while their owners are away

2. an object you buy to remember a place or time

3. a vehicle that travels over water

4. shows the location of roads, cities, and landmarks

7. staying outdoors, even to sleep

8. a period of time where you don't attend school or go to work

13. a place that rents rooms to travelers

14. a vehicle that travels on rails

airplane
boat
camping
car
holiday
hotel
kennel
map
pool
postcard
souvenir
suitcase
tourist
train
umbrella
vacation

Spiders

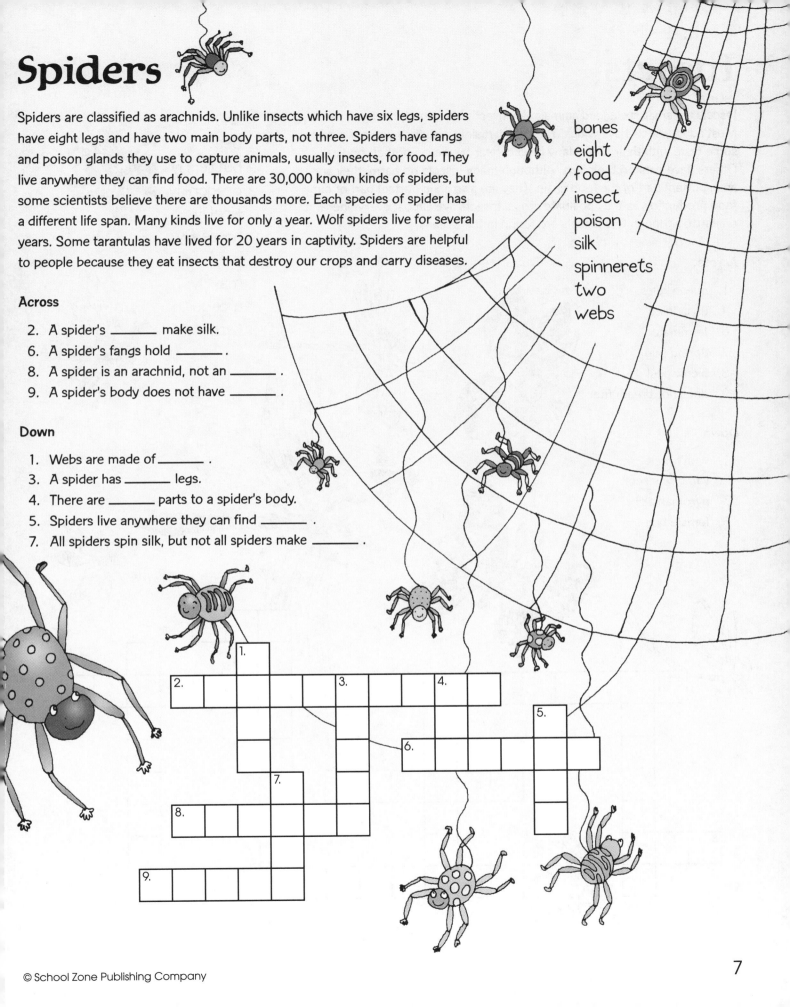

Spiders are classified as arachnids. Unlike insects which have six legs, spiders have eight legs and have two main body parts, not three. Spiders have fangs and poison glands they use to capture animals, usually insects, for food. They live anywhere they can find food. There are 30,000 known kinds of spiders, but some scientists believe there are thousands more. Each species of spider has a different life span. Many kinds live for only a year. Wolf spiders live for several years. Some tarantulas have lived for 20 years in captivity. Spiders are helpful to people because they eat insects that destroy our crops and carry diseases.

bones
eight
food
insect
poison
silk
spinnerets
two
webs

Across

2. A spider's _____ make silk.
6. A spider's fangs hold _____ .
8. A spider is an arachnid, not an _____ .
9. A spider's body does not have _____ .

Down

1. Webs are made of _____ .
3. A spider has _____ legs.
4. There are _____ parts to a spider's body.
5. Spiders live anywhere they can find _____ .
7. All spiders spin silk, but not all spiders make _____ .

7

Insects

Insects are small six-legged animals. An insect's body has three main parts. Most adult insects have wings. They smell mainly with their antennae, and some taste with their feet. Many insects hear by means of their bodies. Others have ears on their legs. Although many insects do harm, they are an important part of the food chain. They are also an important part of our food production as they pollinate crops. Insects live almost everywhere on earth, although few insects are found in the oceans.

ant
bee
butterfly
dragonfly
firefly
horse fly
ladybug
mayfly
mosquito
termite

Across

1. queen rules
4. unsaddled
6. terminator
7. Spring bug
8. picnic pest
9. does not breath fire

Down

1. won't melt
2. vampire insect
3. pyromaniac
5. female bug

Word Sounds

What sounds do they make?
Use the clues to write the words in the puzzle.

Across

Down

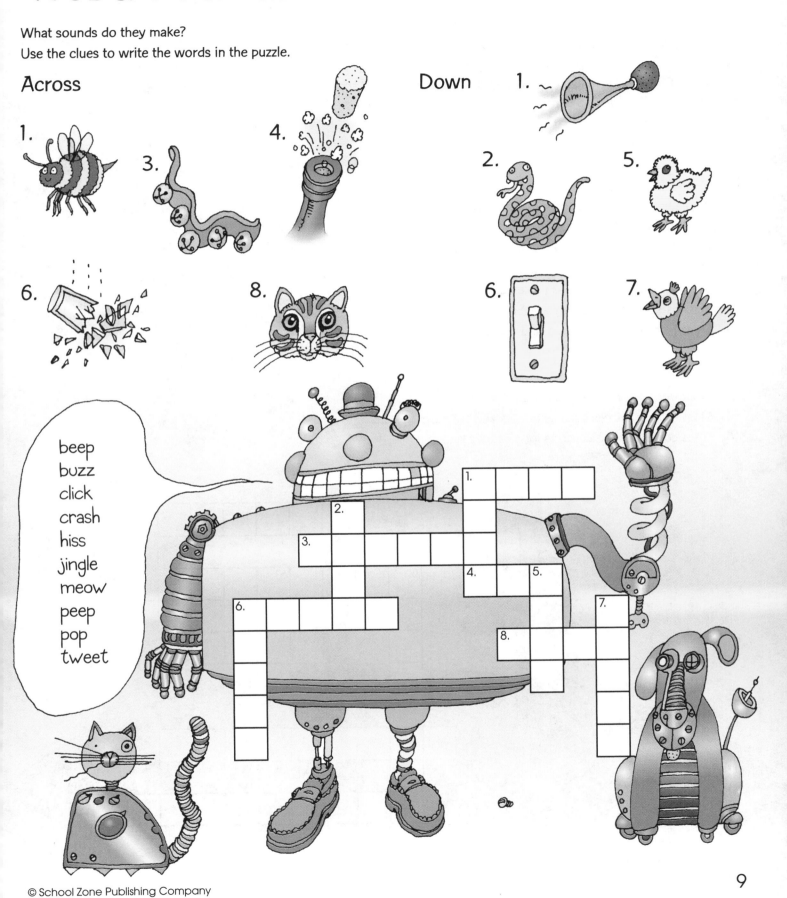

beep
buzz
click
crash
hiss
jingle
meow
peep
pop
tweet

Trees

Trees are the largest of all plants, some of which grow higher than three-story buildings. The giant sequoias of California are the oldest and largest living things. Trees continue to grow as long as they live and some trees live for thousands of years. A tree's leaves make food that helps the tree grow and keeps it alive. Many trees lose their leaves during winter, allowing the trees to rest. Other trees keep their leaves and stay green all year long. There are thousands of kinds of trees, some of which only grow in warm regions.

botanists
deciduous
evergreen
grow
food
roots
seed
soil
water
wood

Across

1. A tree has three main parts: (1) the trunk and branches; (2) the leaves; (3) the _____ .
3. One of the most valuable parts of a tree is _____ .
5. Most needleleaf trees are _____ .
7. The main job of leaves is to make _____ .
8. Scientists who study plants are called _____ .
9. Trees help conserve _____ and _____ .

Down

2. Most trees begin life as a _____ .
4. Most broadleaf trees such as maples and oaks are _____ .
6. Trees continue to _____ as long as they live.

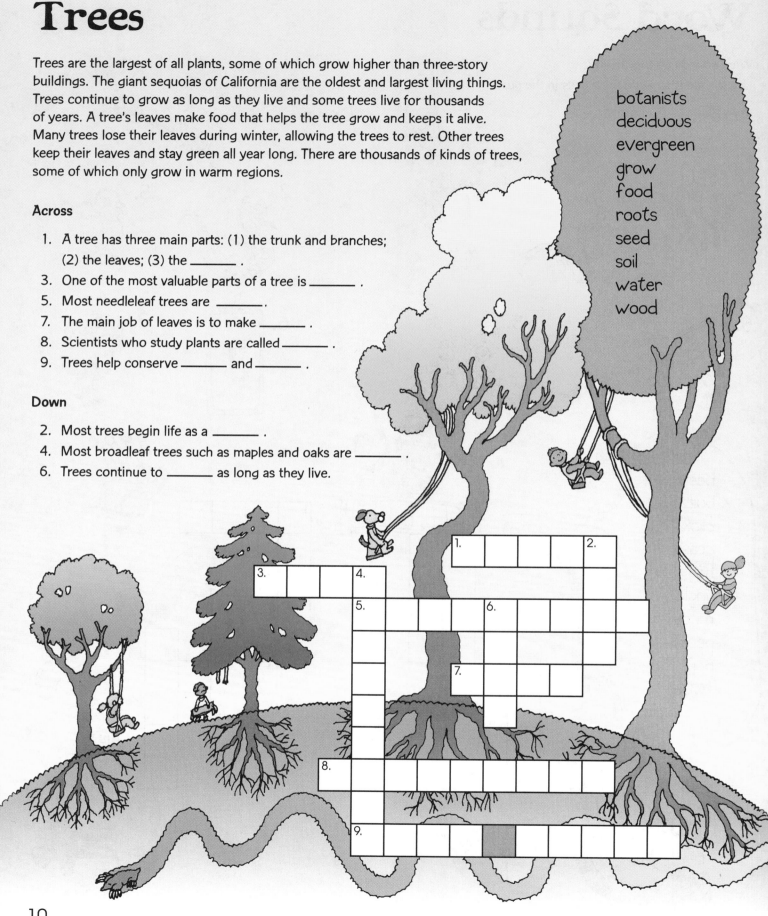

Reptiles

Reptiles include alligators, crocodiles, lizards, snakes, turtles, and the tuatara. Reptiles are cold-blooded, which means their body temperature is about the same as their surroundings. In climates with harsh winters they hibernate. In extremely hot climates they are mainly active at night. Many reptiles live a long time. Some turtles have lived in captivity for more than 100 years. Reptiles live on every continent except Antarctica, and in all the oceans except those in the polar regions. Some reptiles, including lizards, snakes, and crocodiles, are hunted for their skins. The United States government prohibits the import of skins of those reptiles classified as endangered species.

backbone
dinosaur
land
lungs
plates
reptiles
shell
temperature

Across

2. Reptiles breathe air through _____ .
5. Cold-blooded animals do not have a constant body _____ .
7. A spectacular reptile that is now extinct _____ .
8. Most reptiles live on _____ .

Down

1. Reptile skin is made of scales or bony _____ .
3. An animal that is a vertebrate has a _____ .
4. Turtles, snakes, lizards, and crocodiles are all _____ .
6. Turtles are the only reptiles with a _____ .

Word Meaning

Find a word to match each clue. Write the words in the puzzle.

Across

4. speak very softly
5. make a loud cry
7. say funny things
8. talk in a friendly way

Down

1. talk over
2. say out loud
3. talk big
6. share news

brag
chat
discuss
joke
report
scream
speak
whisper

Oceans

There are five oceans that surround the continents. Three of the great world oceans, in order of size, are the Pacific, the Atlantic, and the Indian. These three oceans meet around the continent of Antarctica in the Southern Hemisphere to form the Antarctic Ocean. These three oceans meet again at the top of the earth to form the Arctic Ocean. The word **sea** can name any body of water, from a large lake to an ocean. Connected to each ocean are smaller bodies of water called seas, bays, and gulfs that are defined by land or islands.

Across

3. These are places off a coast where seaweed grows as tall as trees _____ .

6. This fish doesn't look like one.

8. Seaweed doesn't have _____ to take in water.

9. You'll find the most colorful fish here.

Down

1. These form when wind blows across the ocean.

2. This fish looks like its name and stays near the ocean floor.

4. When the tide goes out, ocean water is left here.

5. Skeletons of these tiny animals form coral reefs.

7. The moon and sun cause the _____ .

coral reefs
kelp forests
polyps
rockfish
roots
sea horse
tidal pools
tides
waves

Food Groups

A balanced diet is important for good nutrition. Nutrition is the science that deals with food and how the body uses it. There are five major food groups that nutrition experts recommend: (1) breads, cereals, rice, and pasta; (2) vegetables; (3) fruits; (4) milk, yogurt, and cheese; and (5) meat, poultry, fish, dried beans and peas, eggs, and nuts. Fats and sweets should be eaten in small quantities. A good diet helps prevent certain diseases and supplies the body with the energy needed to perform every action we make. The body needs good nutrition to help maintain all its functions and regulate the body processes.

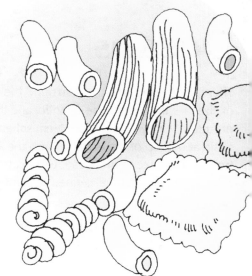

Across

5. You get energy from these in bread, rice, and potatoes.

6. This liquid is good for strong bones and teeth.

7. This is another word for carbohydrates.

8. This oily substance gives you energy and keeps you warm.

9. This comes from ocean water. You sprinkle it on your food.

10. Spaghetti is one kind.

Down

1. It makes food sweet, but too much can cause cavities.

2. These come from plants, often taste sweet, and are good to eat every day.

3. A kind of food that has protein you need to grow.

4. You should eat several servings a day from this food group.

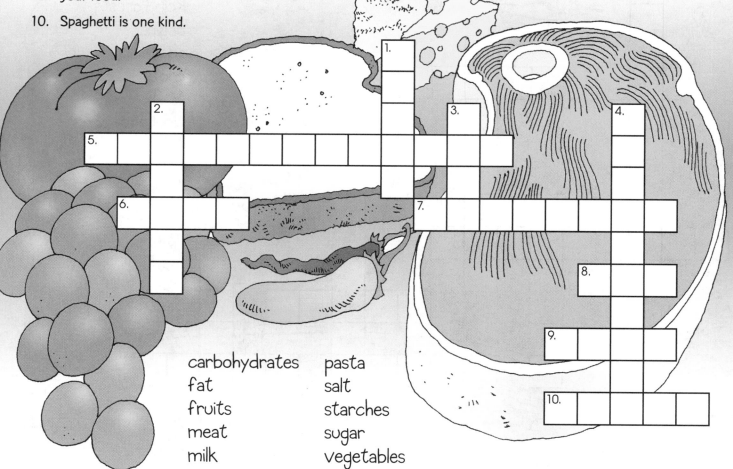

carbohydrates
fat
fruits
meat
milk
pasta
salt
starches
sugar
vegetables

14

Bees

Bees are one of the most useful insects. During food-gathering, bees spread pollen from one flower to another. Many food crops, including fruits and vegetables, depend on bees for fertilization. They also produce honey, which people use as food, and beeswax that is used in candles, cosmetics, and other products. They live in almost every part of the world except the North and South Poles.

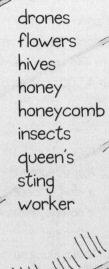

drones
flowers
hives
honey
honeycomb
insects
queen's
sting
worker

Across

3. The _____ is used to raise young bees and to store nectar.

6. _____ provide food for bees.

8. Bees are _____ .

Down

1. The only function of the _____ is to mate with queens.

2. The job of the _____ honey bees is to collect nectar and pollen from flowers.

3. Only the kinds known as _____ bees make honey in large enough amounts to be used by people.

4. Honey bees live in _____ in a colony made up of one queen, tens of thousands of workers, and a few hundred drones.

5. Laying eggs is the _____ only job.

7. Most bees depend on their _____ for defense.

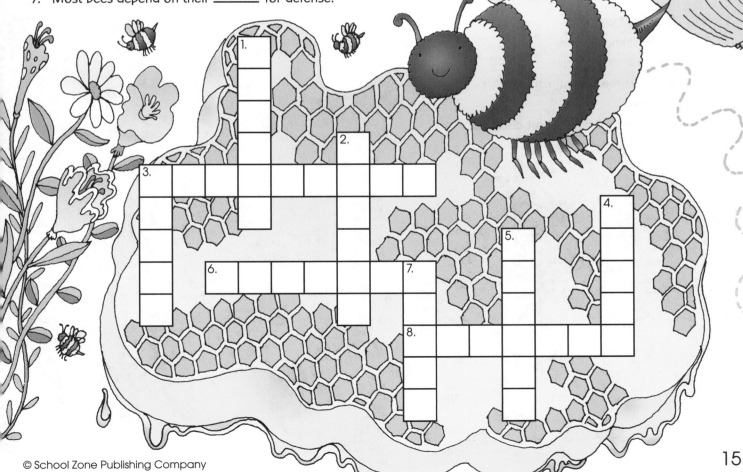

Mammals

Mammals differ from most other animals in five important ways. Mother mammals feed milk from their own bodies to their young. Only mammals have hair for part or all of their lives. Mammals are warm-blooded. The temperature of their body stays the same no matter how hot or cold the weather. Mammals have a larger, more well-developed brain than other animals. Mammals care for their young. They protect them and teach them the skills they will need to live on their own. There are more than 4,500 species of mammals and they live almost everywhere.

Across

1. longest neck
5. flying mammal
6. a kind of deer
7. a cowboy rides one
9. feline pet
10. looks like a striped horse
11. scared Red Riding Hood
13. third largest land animal

Down

1. Billy Goat Gruff was one
2. Peter is a well-known one
3. carries a trunk
4. the blue one is the largest mammal
8. wears a mask
9. fastest running animal for short distances
12. known as sly

bat
cat
cheetah
elephant
elk
fox
giraffe
goat
hippo
horse
rabbit
raccoon
whale
wolf
zebra

17

Homes

Write the words in the puzzle. Then circle the words on the list that name different kinds of home words.

apartment
cabin
castle
cottage
door
floor
houseboat
igloo
roof
teepee
walls

1. C

2. W
3. C
4. A
5. T
6. D
7. H
8. R
9. F
10. I

Habitats

The place where an animal lives is called its habitat. There are seven major types of habitats: mountains, grasslands, temperate forests, tropical forests, deserts, polar regions, and oceans. Each habitat supports many kinds of animals. Most of these animals have lived in the same surroundings for centuries and have adapted to the climate. No single species of animal can survive everywhere. Habitats that are being destroyed, such as the rain forest, cause the death of many animals as they have lost their homes and source of food. Living things depend on one another. If all the trees in an area are cut down, the animals that depend on them will die.

Across

2. The _____ _____ exist in very hot and humid parts of the world where the temperature is relatively constant.

4. Plants and animals that live in the ocean live in _____ .

8. An _____ is home to fish and mammals.

10. Marshes, bogs, and swamps are all kinds of _____ .

Down

1. _____ are wide areas covered with grasses and trees.

3. A _____ is a very dry place that receives very little rainfall and can support little vegetation. Not all are hot.

5. The _____ is a huge treeless plain that reaches from the Arctic Ocean to where the northern forests begin.

6. A deciduous _____ has trees that shed their leaves in autumn.

7. Most lakes, rivers, and _____ are fresh water.

9. _____ are wetlands that are flooded all the time.

desert
forest
grasslands
ocean
ponds
rain forests
salt water
swamps
tundra
wetland

19

Circus

Circus-type performers go back thousands of years. In ancient Rome, part of the entertainment featured chariot races with men standing on the bare backs of two horses racing around the track. During the Middle Ages, jesters and other performers entertained on the streets or royal courts. The golden age of circuses in America began about 1870. A variety of performers, including aerialists, acrobats, clowns, dancers, musicians, and trained animals, performed under a tent called the Big Top. Today, most circuses are held in tents and arenas around the world.

acrobats
band
Big Top
clowns
costumes
elephants
horses
jugglers
parade
rings
roustabouts
tigers
trapeze
tricks

Across

2. _____ wear bright velvet or satin ornaments and may have a pretty girl perched on their heads. Many are taught to do tricks.

5. _____ perform stunts, sometimes while on a cantering horse.

8. Aerialists perform while on a high _____ .

9. Trained _____ canter while riders jump from one to another.

10. _____ use a variety of objects such as dishes or even flaming torches.

11. _____ unload equipment, set it up, and take it down after the last performance.

13. Circuses once took place under a tent called the _____ _____ .

Down

1. The circus _____ plays throughout the performance and sets the tempo for the acts.

3. Some circuses have a _____ where performers and animals march around the arena.

4. Different acts take place at the same time in different _____ .

6. All circus performers wear bright _____ .

7. _____ in funny costumes and comic makeup entertain the audience with playful antics and tricks.

8. _____ perform tricks while inside a wire cage with their trainer.

12. Both animals and clowns perform entertaining _____ .

20

Ball Games

Across

3. Ping-Pong
5. not hardball
6. tenpins
9. pointy ball

Down

1. hands only
2. began with a bushel
3. what a racket
4. not a vegetable
6. fast ball
7. putter around
8. heads up

baseball
basketball
bowling
football
golf
soccer
softball
squash
table tennis
tennis
volleyball

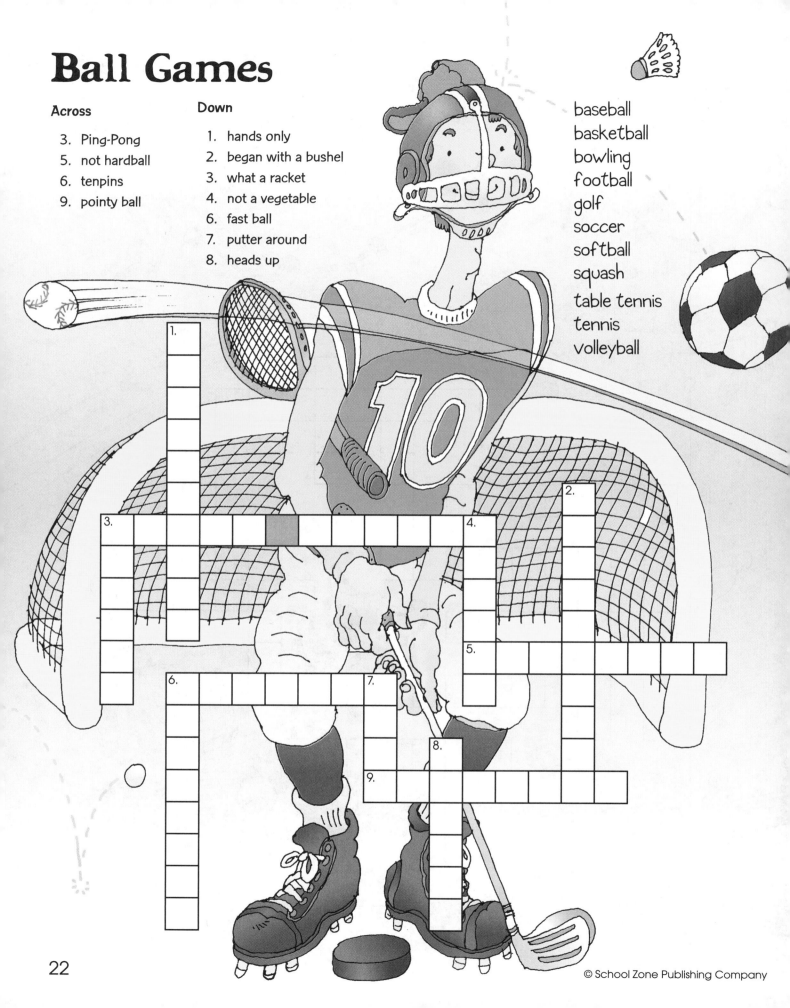

Cold Weather Mammals

Animals that live in icy conditions have evolved in different ways to cope. Mammals such as the polar bears have thick coats of long, shaggy hair and a fleecy layer of fur closer to their skin. Whales, polar bears, and seals have thick layers of fat under their skin. Birds that live in polar regions have thick plumage and fluff out their feathers to help keep them warm. To be able to walk across the snow easily, bears have developed big, wide feet that act like snowshoes and birds such as ptarmigan and grouse have feathers on the soles of their feet. Animals that live in the polar regions are in sub-zero temperatures and total darkness for up to nine months during winter.

Across

3. Layers of _____ help keep some mammals warm.

5. The white bear of the frozen Arctic is called the _____ _____ .

7. Walrus _____ is tough and waterproof.

9. The mountain goat's hoofs are _____ on the bottom.

10. The polar bear uses its _____ legs to pull itself through the water.

Down

1. A mammal with tusks that is related to seals is the _____ .

2. Thick _____ keeps some mammals warm.

4. Mountain sheep and goats have sharp _____ .

6. Some mammals sleep all winter, or _____ .

8. In the Arctic, temperatures below _____ are not unusual.

fat
front
fur
hibernate
hoofs
polar bear
rubbery
skin
walrus
zero

Board Games

There is a great variety of board games, and each year many new board games appear on the market. Both children and adults enjoy games, whether for the challenge of perfecting a skill, the excitement of competition, or simply for fun. One of the oldest known board games has been dated by archaeologists to be 4,500 years old. Some board games require skill and strategy, and some are games of chance. Board game categories include trivia games, word games, games of logic and deduction, and financial games.

Across

2. strategy game known to be at least 4,300 years old and very popular in China, Japan, and Korea
3. game based on knowledge of an array of subjects
4. often a child's first board game
5. one of the oldest strategy games played to capture the opponent's king
7. child's game of chance played with spinner to determine moves
8. detective game

Down

1. game using play money to buy and sell real estate
4. game similar to chess, the object of which is to capture the opponent's men
6. word game that requires spelling and vocabulary skills

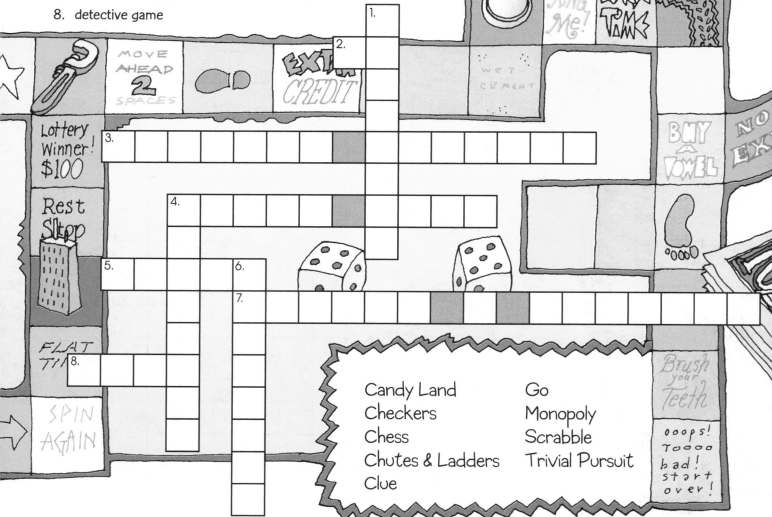

Candy Land
Checkers
Chess
Chutes & Ladders
Clue
Go
Monopoly
Scrabble
Trivial Pursuit

Sports

Sports are organized athletic activities played by individuals or in teams. Sports are played for fun, exercise, or competition. There are different types of sports. Individual sports do not require a group or team of players. Combative sports set one person against another as in boxing. Outdoor sports such as camping involve people in nature. Team sports, including football and basketball, require players to communicate and work together. Many people participate in amateur sports such as organized softball leagues. Professional athletes participate in sports as careers.

baseball
basketball
bowling
football
golf
hockey
skateboarding
snowboarding
soccer
squash
tennis

Across

1. downhill slide
3. it's a kick
5. love for two
7. batter up
9. pucker up
10. small ball

Down

1. free wheeling
2. dunk it
4. tenpins
6. get your quarter back
8. not a veggie

Natural Disasters

Natural disasters are sudden and extremely unfortunate events that affect many people. Meteorologists study weather and the earth to predict and understand natural disasters. Different parts of the world have different kinds of disasters. Avalanches are huge drifts of snow that rush downward. Volcanoes erupt hot gases and melted rock from miles below the earth's surface. Tornadoes, hurricanes, and typhoons are caused by tremendous winds. Earthquakes result from moving plates deep in the earth. Tsunamis are huge ocean waves caused by undersea earthquakes or volcanoes.

avalanche
blizzard
cyclones
earthquake
flood
hurricane
tornado
tsunami
typhoons

Across

3. a huge downward drift of snow

5. violent, rotating winds that form a funnel cloud that can destroy almost everything in its path when it touches ground

7. a violent motion of the earth's surface caused by volcanoes or rock movement below the earth's surface

8. a powerful storm that develops over warm water with a calm area in the center and winds that swirl around the eye

Down

1. hurricanes near Australia and in the Indian Oceans are called _____

2. a blinding snowstorm with strong, cold winds

4. the overflow of water on land where people live caused by too much rain or melting snow

5. huge ocean waves caused by undersea earthquakes or volcanoes

6. hurricanes are called _____ in the Western Pacific Ocean and South China Seas

Sea Mammals

Until 1758, whales were regarded as fish. Though resembling some of the large sharks, they have all the attributes of mammals. They breathe air with lungs, they give birth to living young that are nursed on the mother's milk, and they guard their young. Whales are found in all oceans. Walruses inhabit only the Arctic Ocean and adjacent ice-covered seas. In the quest for their ivory tusks and thick hide for oil, Europeans nearly eliminated the walrus from the Arctic almost 100 years ago. Seals generally live along the continental coasts and islands. Most types of seals live in the earth's polar and temperate zones, where fish populations are largest.

blowhole
blue
mammals
salt
seals
steer
surface
walrus
water

Across

2. Ocean water is _____ water.
3. Whales use flippers to balance and _____ .
5. Whales and dolphins are _____ .
7. Dolphins breath out a _____ .
8. Sea lions and _____ spend much of their life in water.

Down

1. Over two-thirds of Earth is covered by_____ .
3. Dolphins and whales come to the _____ to breathe.
4. Scientists classify the _____ as a kind of large seal.
6. The _____ whale is the largest animal on Earth.

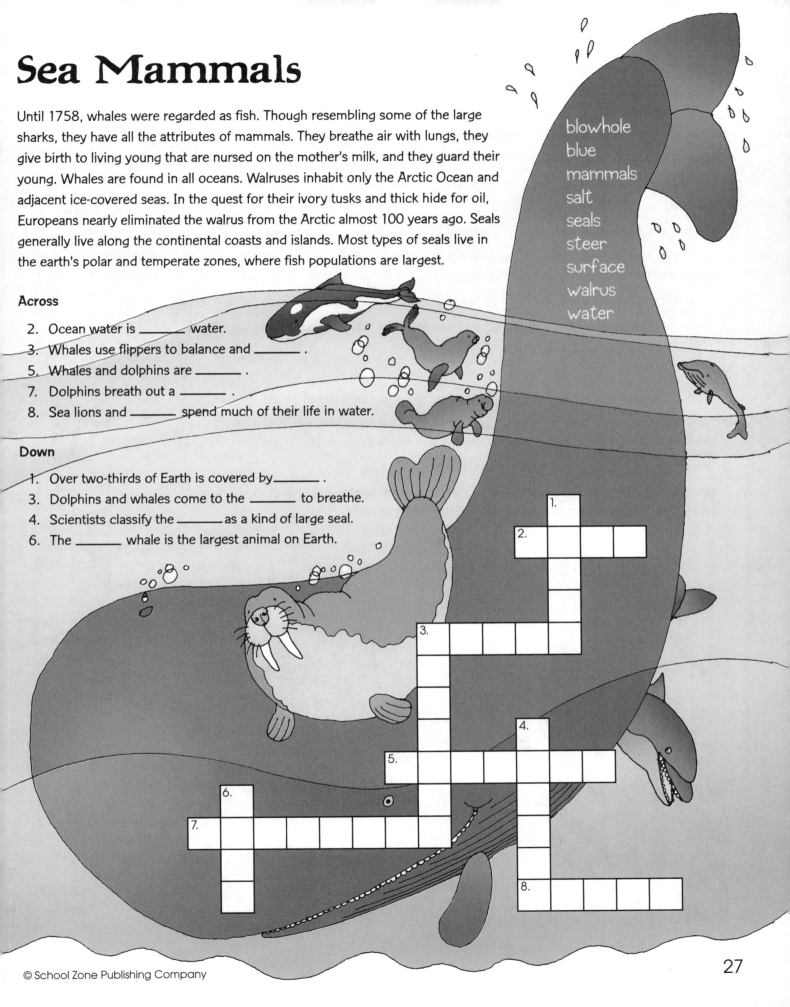

Inventors

Inventing is putting ideas and materials together to make something that did not exist before. Inventions have been occurring since the Stone Age, when people began using rocks as tools. New inventions can make life easier, healthier, more comfortable, and fun.

Benz
Daimler
Edison
Franklin
Graham Bell
Gutenberg
Kellogg
Lister
Wright

Across

3. In the mid 1400s, Johannes _____ invented printing as we know it today.

5. In 1865, Joseph _____ began the use of antiseptics during surgery, which almost eliminated post-surgical infection.

6. The electric light bulb was invented by Thomas _____ in the late 1800s.

7. A breakfast cereal still produced today was developed by Will _____ in the 1890s.

Down

1. The _____ brothers are credited with the first real airplane flights in 1903.

2. In 1885, Karl _____ and Gottlieb _____ built the first internal-combustion engines that were basically the same as the gasoline engines used in cars today.

3. Alexander_____ _____ patented the telephone in 1876.

4. In 1752, Benjamin _____ flew a kite in a thunderstorm to prove lightning was electrical, which led to his invention of the lightning rod.

28

29

Holidays

Each state has the authority to specify the holidays it will observe. The president and Congress designate the holidays to be observed in Washington D. C., and by federal employees throughout the country. Banks and schools usually close on a legal holiday. When a holiday falls on Sunday, it is usually observed on the following Monday. Some traditional holidays are observed by schools and organizations, although the schools and organizations do not close.

January
February
May
July
September
October
November
December

Across

4. Washington's Birthday
6. Independence Day
7. Thanksgiving
8. Christmas

Down

1. Memorial Day
2. Labor Day
3. New Year's Day
5. Columbus Day

30

Birds

If it has feathers, it's a bird. All birds have feathers and all birds have wings. But not all birds fly. Ostriches walk or run and penguins use their wings for balance when they walk or as flippers when they swim. Birds hatch from eggs. There are about 9,700 kinds of birds. The fastest birds can fly at speeds over 100 miles an hour. No other animal can travel faster than birds. Birds are important to man in many ways. They scatter seeds, pollinate flowers, eat harmful insects, and are an important source of food for people. Birds live all over the world, from the polar regions to the tropics.

cones
down
frogs
hummingbirds
molt
oil
straight
toes

Across

4. Birds have _____ that keeps their feathers dry.
5. These birds can fly backward.
8. Ostriches have two big _____ .

Down

1. Herons eat fish and _____ .
2. These feathers keep birds warm.
3. The bottom of a bird's wing is _____ .
6. When birds _____ , they lose feathers a few at a time.
7. Seed-eating birds have beaks shaped like this.

United States Facts

Until the 1500s, what is now the United States was once a wilderness. Indians in various groups lived scattered over the land between the Atlantic and Pacific Oceans. During the 1600s people from England and other European countries began settling along the East Coast. By 1776, the colonists established an independent nation. Today, the United States is the third largest country in the world. It is the fourth largest in population.

Alaska
Atlantic
California
fifty
Lake Michigan
Mississippi
New York
Pacific
Rhode Island
Wyoming

Across

4. largest lake within the U.S. borders
6. the number of states in the U.S.
7. least populated state
8. most populated state
10. smallest state

Down

1. the ocean on the West Coast
2. the largest state
3. the longest river
5. the largest city
9. the ocean on the East Coast

Tennis

Across

1. Tennis is a game played with one or two opposing _____ .

7. A _____ is used to hit the ball.

9. A zero score is called _____ .

10. A game of _____ is played with four people.

11. To win a _____ a player or team must win six games and lead by at least two games.

12. A _____ is stretched across the middle of the court.

Down

1. A _____ is won when the opposing side fails to return the ball or makes an error.

2. A serve that cannot be returned is an _____ .

3. _____ is a game played with two opposing people.

4. A 40-40 tie is called _____ .

5. The _____ puts the ball in play.

6. Rackets are used to hit the _____ back and forth over a net.

8. Tennis is played on a flat surface called a _____ .

ace
ball
court
deuce
doubles
love
net
players
point
racket
service
set
singles

34

Math Vocabulary

Write the definitions of the items in red to solve the puzzle.

Across

b. $3\overline{)9}$ with 3 above

d. $\frac{4}{5}$

g. $3/4$

h. $3\overline{)12}$ with 4 above

i. $7 \times 8 = 56$

j. ▦ ▦ ▦

k. $4 \times 6 = 24$

Down

a. $\begin{array}{r} 3 \\ +4 \\ \hline 7 \end{array}$

c. $9/10$

e. $3\overline{)10}$ with 3 above, 9 and 1 below

f. $\begin{array}{r} 12 \\ -6 \\ \hline 6 \end{array}$

g. $2\overline{)18}$ with 9 above

Word bank:
denominator
difference
dividend
divisor
factors
fraction
numerator
product
quotient
remainder
sets
sum

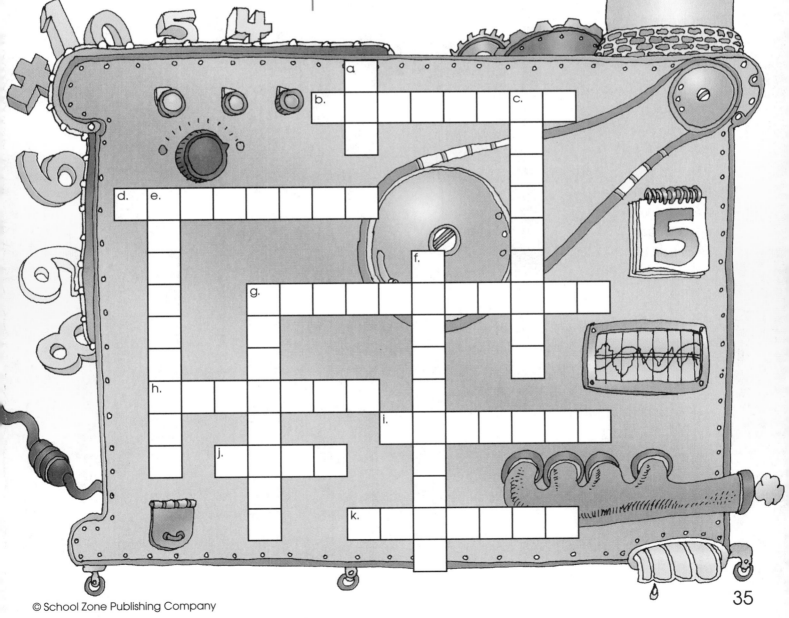

Name That Dog

People have had dogs as pets for over 10,000 years. Most scientists believe that prehistoric man first valued dogs as watchdogs. Dogs eventually became used for herding and hunting other animals. Over thousands of years, different breeds were developed for certain tasks. Some breeds were developed to herd sheep, goats, and cattle. Others were bred for various kinds of hunting. Many kinds of toy dogs were developed to provide company for people. Dogs perform many important tasks for people. Police use dogs to track criminals and sniff out illegal drugs and hidden explosives. They also lead the blind and serve as "ears" for deaf people. Many dogs have been trained to perform in circuses and in motion pictures.

Afghan
Beagle
Boxer
Dachshund
Dalmation
Great Dane
Greyhound
Husky
Pointer
Poodle
Retriever
Setter

Across

2. not a bus
6. go fetch dog
7. not a sitter
8. long, silky hair
10. does not wear gloves
11. think fire truck

Down

1. looks like a wolf
2. BIG
3. nickname, hot dog
4. points the way
5. rabbit chaser
9. fancy haircuts

36

Land Transportation

Land transportation is the most common kind of transportation by far. Automobiles, buses, motorcycles, snowmobiles, trains, and trucks are the chief engine-powered vehicles. Cars, buses, and trucks are the main road vehicles. Routes are predetermined for buses, and trains and subways that run on tracks. Trucks can deliver freight to where it is needed. Cars allow people to choose their routes. Cars consume more than half the energy used for transportation in the United States and are a major source of traffic congestion and pollution problems in cities and towns. The U.S. government has established pollution-control standards and fuel-consumption standards to help reduce these problems.

automobile
bicycle
bus
motorcycle
streetcar
subway
taxicab
train
truck

Across

2. an underground train
4. a chauffeur-driven car for hire
5. a two-wheeled—sometimes with a third for a side car—automotive vehicle
7. a two-wheeled vehicle propelled by pedaling
8. a vehicle designed to move heavy objects

Down

1. a vehicle by which most families travel
2. rides on rails and transports passengers on city streets
3. a large passenger vehicle
6. a connected line of cars that ride on rails, pulled by a locomotive

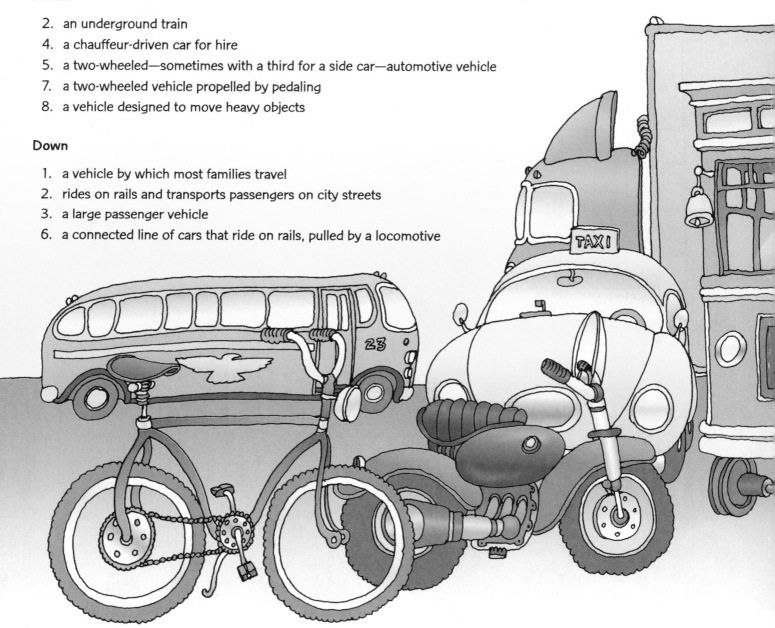

38

Airports

Across

1. people who buy tickets to travel by plane
3. where air traffic controllers direct air traffic near the airport and movement on the ground
6. paper that shows you have paid and where you are going
7. buildings in which aircraft are stored and repaired
8. where passengers board and leave aircraft from terminal locations
10. what must be inspected by security employees

Down

1. a person qualified to operate an airplane
2. enforce security regulations set up by the FAA
4. roads for planes to take off and land
5. the main airport building for passengers and services
9. provides energy and power to engines

baggage
control tower
fuel
gate
hangars
passengers
pilot
runways
security guards
terminal
tickets

40

Shape Words

Write the names of the figures in the puzzle.

Across

5.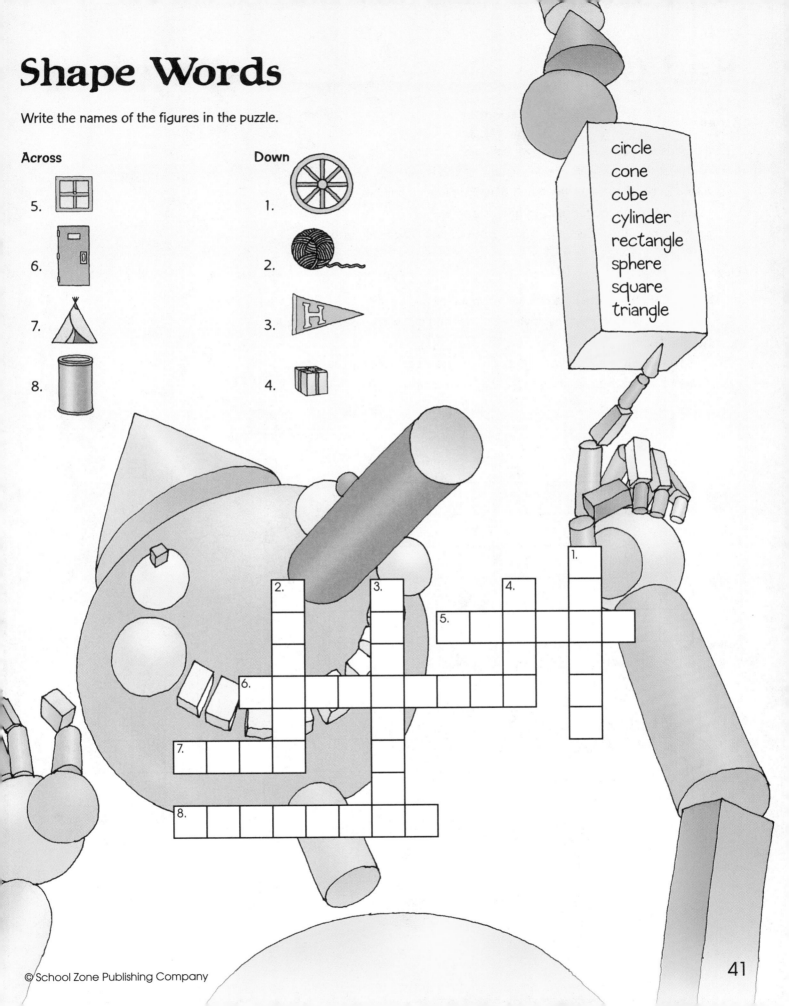

6.

7.

8.

Down

1.

2.

3.

4.

circle
cone
cube
cylinder
rectangle
sphere
square
triangle

Bad Guys

Across

1. a bloodsucking insect that carries diseases such as malaria
3. an insect that invades homes, restaurants, and warehouses, spoiling food
5. a kind of bat that drinks the blood of warm-blooded animals
6. pests that live in the fur of dogs and cats
9. caterpillars of this insect strip leaves from trees, killing many of them

Down

2. an arachnid that has a poisonous sting in its tail
4. a common, winged pest that invades homes and can carry diseases such as typhoid fever
7. these ant-like insects eat wood in our homes and can cause great damage
8. a rodent that carries diseases and will attack humans

cockroach
fleas
gypsy moth
housefly
mosquito
rat
scorpion
termites
vampire

What Makes Weather?

Weather takes place in the atmosphere, the layer of air that surrounds the earth. Most weather occurs from the earth's surface up to an altitude of about 6 to 10 miles. Three factors determine the weather. **Air temperature**, which is the measure of warmth; **air pressure**, which affects wind; and **humidity**, a measure of the amount of water vapor in the air. There are all kinds of weather—rain, snow, sun, wind, fog, frost. All of them are changes in the air caused by the varying effect of the sun's warmth. Winds blow, for instance, when the sun heats some places more than others, causing air to move. Rain falls when air warmed by the sun causes enough evaporation to form big drops of water when it condenses. Weather affects people's lives every day in all parts of the world.

air pressure
condensation
evaporation
precipitation
temperature
water
weather
wind

Across

1. A thermometer measures _____ .
3. What we wear depends on the _____ .
7. Rain, snow, and hail are kinds of _____ .
8. Drops of water on a cold can are _____ .

Down

2. _____ is what happens when water turns to water vapor.
4. The push of air on the earth is _____ _____ .
5. Cold air can't hold as much _____ as warm air can.
6. Moving air is _____ .

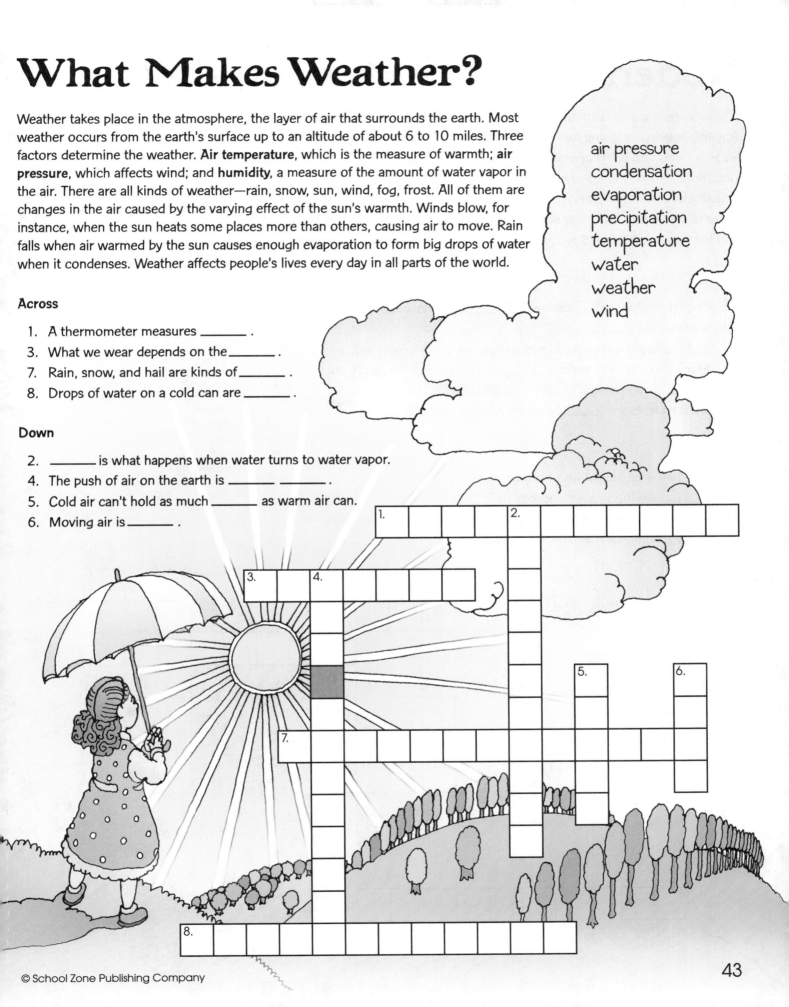

Rodents

Rodents are mammals with front teeth especially suited to gnawing hard objects. Rodents have two top and two bottom front teeth. They wear away at the tips but do not wear out until late in the animal's lifetime as they keep growing until the animal becomes old. There are many kinds of rodents. They are both helpful and harmful to people. Scientists use mice and rats for research. Some rodents eat harmful insects and weeds. Beavers, chinchillas, and other rodents have valuable fur. But serious diseases, such as typhus and the plague, are carried by rodents. Some rodents cause damage to crops and property.

capybaras
diseases
fur
rodents
gnawing
grow
herbivorous
mammals
mice
scientists

Across

1. The teeth of rodents continue to _____ until the animal is very old.
2. Rodents are _____ .
4. _____ are the largest rodents and can be up to 4 feet long.
5. Many rodents carry serious _____ such as the plague and typhus.
6. _____ live in almost all parts of the world.
8. Most rodents are _____ (plant eaters).

Down

1. A rodent is an animal with front teeth especially suited to _____ hard objects.
2. _____ are the smallest rodents.
3. Rats and mice are helpful to _____ , who use them for research.
7. Some rodents such as chinchilla rabbits have valuable _____ .

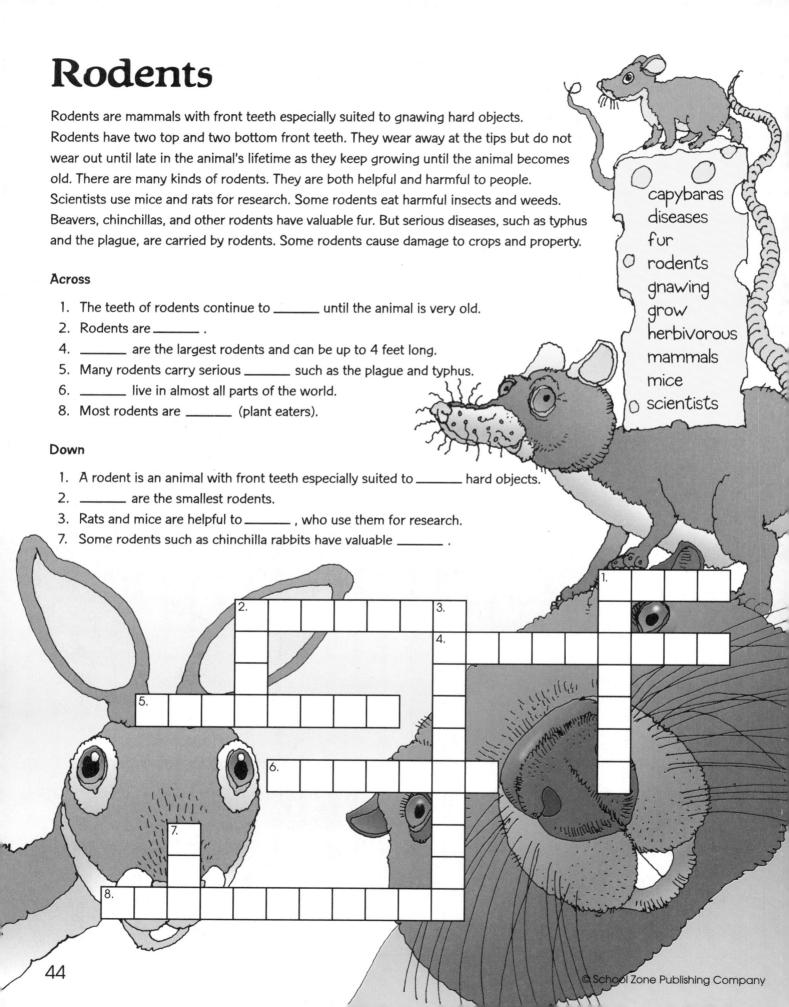

Baseball

Across

2. A _____ throws the ball for the player at bat.
6. The approximate shape of the infield is a _____ .
7. A _____ is a long, rounded wooden stick used to hit the ball.
8. Home plate has _____ sides.
9. An _____ calls balls and strikes.
11. Each _____ marks a corner of the diamond that runners must touch to score a run.
13. The _____ is the area of the baseball field that is outside the infield.
14. Defensive players wear a _____ on one hand.

Down

1. A _____ is called when a batter swings and misses.
3. The batter stands at _____ plate.
4. A player who moves from third base to cross home plate scores a _____ .
5. A _____ catches the balls that pass the batter.
8. A ball that is batted high into the air is called a _____ .
10. An _____ is a division of the game in which both teams have a turn at bat and in the field.
12. The American and National League pennant winners play one another in the World _____ .
13. A team's turn at bat is over after three _____ .

base
bat
catcher
diamond
five
fly ball
glove
home
inning
outfield
outs
pitcher
run
Series
strike
umpire

Ecosystems

Different parts of the world support a wide variety of plant and animal life. This is mainly caused by the climate in each place, which allows different kinds of living things to thrive. The climate is influenced by the physical characteristics of a region—whether it is mountainous or near the sea, for example—and its position on Earth. Similar conditions exist in different parts of the world even if they are thousands of miles apart. Each area contains communities of living things that rely on each other for survival. These communities are called ecosystems.

Across

2. An animal that eats flesh of another animal is a _____ .
4. Evaporation, condensation, and precipitation are the three steps to the _____ _____ .
6. The environment in which a species lives .
7. _____ is the study of how plants and animals interact.
8. An animal that eats plants is a _____ .
9. Animals that eat both plants and animals are _____ .
10. The study of plants is called _____ .

Down

1. A _____ is a plant or animal that lives in or on another plant or animal for its only source of food.
3. _____ is the science of weather.
5. Plants and animals need water and _____ to live.

botany
carnivore
ecology
habitat
herbivore
meteorology
omnivores
oxygen
parasite
water cycle

46

Body Systems

The human body has nearly a dozen interrelated systems, each designed for a special function. The skeleton is the framework. Bones provide the system for putting muscular contractions into bodily movements. Oxygen needed to provide fuel for muscles depends on the circulatory system that depends on the respiratory system, and so on with other related systems. Each part of our body does a special job, but all parts work together. What separates people from all other living things is the human brain. Everything you think, feel, and do is controlled by the brain.

blood
brain
ears
eyes
heart
lungs
muscles
skeleton
skin

Across

1. _____ connect with the brain through the optic nerve and are one of our senses.
2. _____ hold and move the skeleton and give the body its shape.
4. The_____ and blood circulation are the major elements of the body's internal transportation system.
5. _____ draw air into the body through the mouth and nose so that oxygen can be absorbed into the bloodstream.
7. The_____ is an outgrowth at the top of the spinal cord and is the organ of thought and neural coordination.

Down

1. _____ are located at the sides of the head and are concerned with the senses of learning and balance.
3. The_____ is the framework around which the body is built.
6. _____ is what the whole body is enclosed in and forms the body's largest organ.
7. _____ contains food, fuel, and materials for building and repairing cells vital to every tissue of the body.

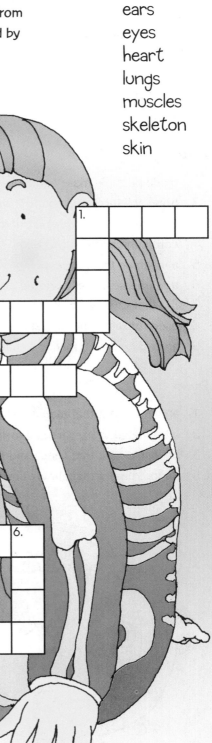

Great Inventions

Invention is the creation of a new device or process or product. It may be the creation of something new or an improvement of something that someone else had produced. Invention is closely related to discovery. Discoverers usually find something that has always existed. For example, people discovered fire, but they invented the match to start a fire. If we compare our homes today with the homes of pioneers, you will appreciate the many inventions that have made our lives easier. Inventions can be beneficial to people, but they can also be harmful. Weapons of war are far more destructive than they once were. People invent to satisfy the needs of people, to make money, or meet military needs. Many inventions fail because they do not fill a need.

airplane
camera
clock
computer
map
microscope
plow
printing press
satellite
telephone
television
wheel

Across

2. made possible mass communication before radio
3. brings pictures and sound from around the world
4. any body that revolves around a planet—artificial ones used for communication and research
5. a machine that processes information with great speed and precision
6. a reference, usually printed, to help people find a destination
7. the first one was probably a potter's table
8. used for taking photographs or making movies
9. an engine-driven machine that can fly

Down

1. an instrument that magnifies extremely small objects
2. a tool used to prepare soil for planting
3. an instrument that sends and receives sound, usually by electricity
5. an instrument that shows time

48

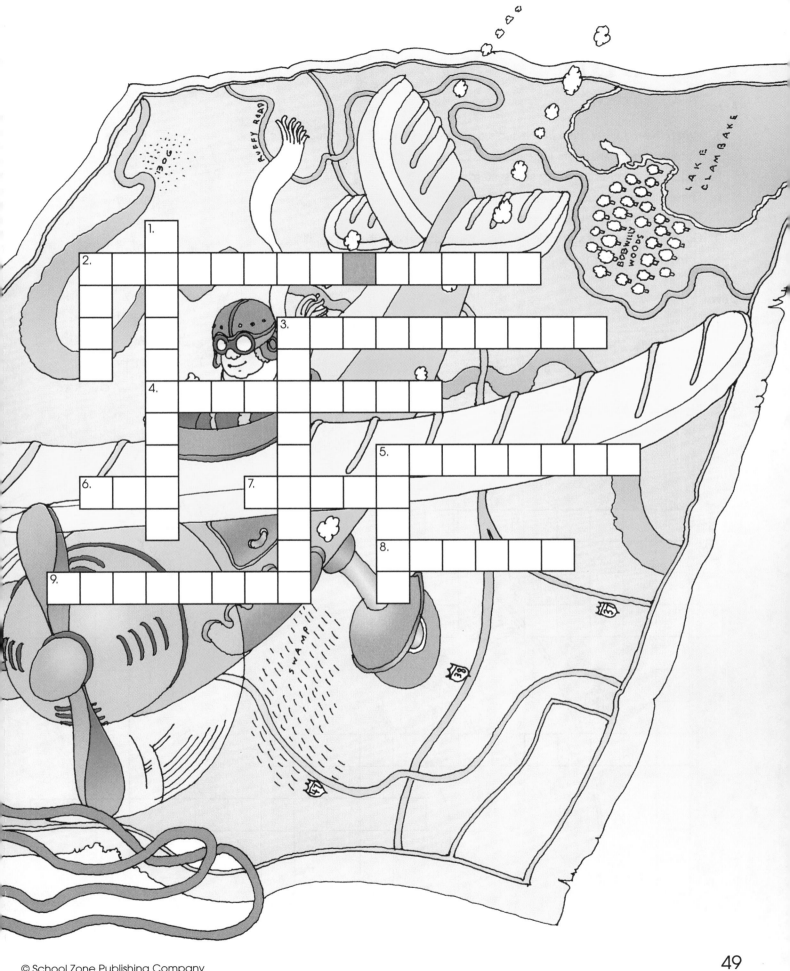

Our Sun

Across

1. When the magnetic field in the sun's core prevents heat from rising to the surface, these dark spots appear: _____ .
5. _____ is another word for star system.
6. There can be no _____ without the sun.
7. The sun shines because it gives out _____ and _____ .
10. Our sun is a type of star called a _____ _____ because it is small compared to other types and gives off a yellow light.

Down

1. _____ _____ are huge eruptions of flames that appear on the sun's surface.
2. A _____ is a huge ball of gas that gives off vast amounts of light and heat.
3. A star is made of _____ and has no solid surface.
4. Our galaxy is named the _____ _____ .
8. Light and heat are forms of _____ .
9. The center of the sun is its _____ .

core
energy
galaxy
gas
light & heat
life
Milky Way
solar flares
star
sunspots
yellow dwarf

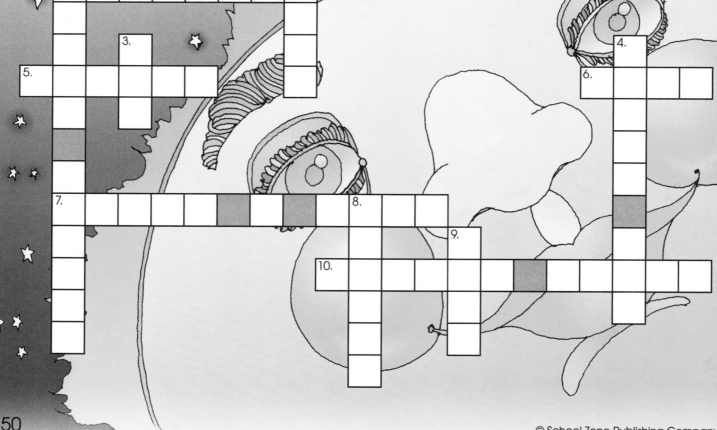

Parts of Speech

The eight ways in which words are used are called the eight parts of speech. A word must be used in a sentence before one can determine which part of speech it is.

Across

2. _____ take the place of nouns.
5. _____ are the name of anything.
6. _____ express strong feeling.
7. _____ modify a verb, an adjective, or another adverb.

Down

1. _____ connect words, phrases, and clauses.
2. _____ show a relationship between its object and another word in the sentence.
3. _____ modify a noun or a pronoun.
4. _____ express action or a state of being.

adjectives
adverbs
conjunctions
interjections
nouns
prepositions
pronouns
verbs

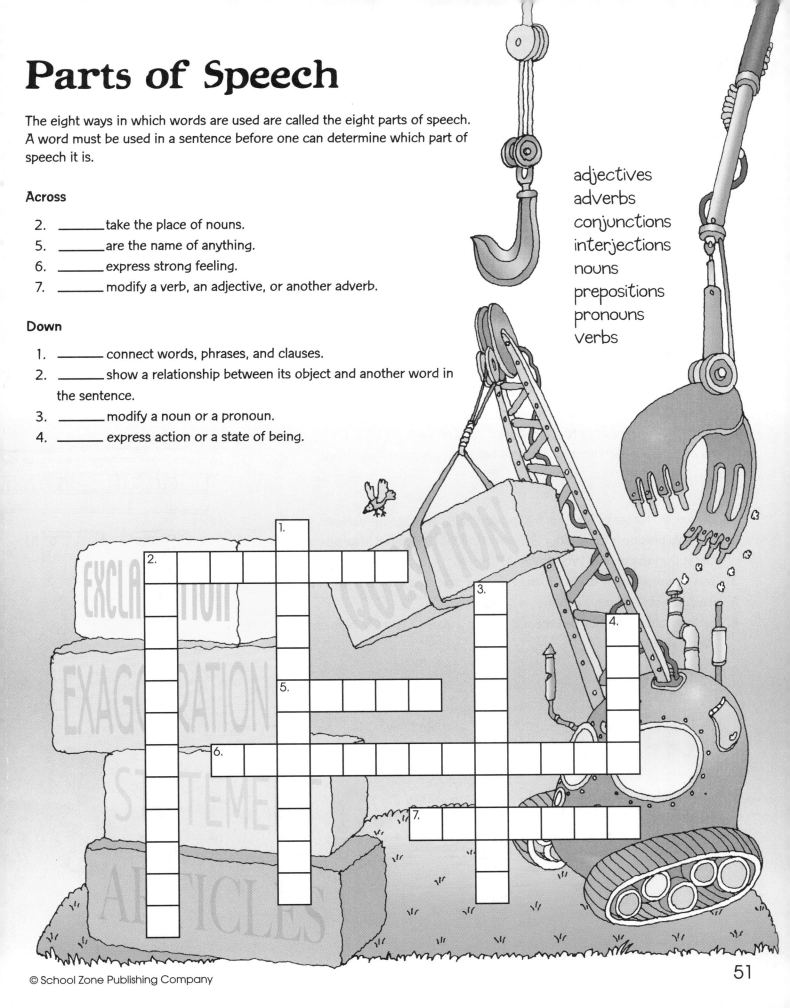

Presidents

The president of the United States is the head of state and chief executive of the country. The Constitution of the United States gives the president enormous power, but also limits that power. He is the commander in chief of the armed forces, decides foreign policy, and can attempt to have new laws passed. In times of emergency, he can give executive orders, laws that do not have to be passed by Congress. He is also limited by the Constitution to provide "checks" on his power. Congress can overturn his decisions if they think his decisions are wrong.

Clinton
F.D. Roosevelt
Ford
G.W. Bush
Jefferson
Kennedy
Lincoln
Nixon
Reagan
T. Roosevelt
Truman
Washington
Wilson

Across

1. proposed the League of Nations, an organization for international cooperation
4. the youngest <u>elected</u> president and the first Catholic to be elected
5. won a controversial election in 2001
7. was president during the Civil War and wrote the Gettysburg Address
8. his domestic policies, called the Square Deal, broke up business monopolies
9. a former actor who became president
10. became president after Nixon resigned from office
11. faced with impeachment for criminal behavior, resigned from office

Down

1. known as "Father of his Country", whose home was Mount Vernon
2. the only president to win four elections...guided the United States through the Great Depression and World War II
3. was responsible for the Louisiana Purchase and the Lewis & Clark expedition
6. was impeached for misconduct in 1999
8. ordered atomic bombs be dropped on two Japanese cities to help end World War II

Motion Pictures

Across

1. supervises the camera crew and lighting for the movie
2. turns a story or idea into a screenplay
3. chooses the director and creative team and controls the budget
5. nonfiction movies that present factual information in a dramatic and entertaining way
8. designs and creates sets and oversees their construction
9. an award given for an outstanding achievement in film making

Down

1. designs and makes the costumes
4. guides the creative efforts of the screenwriter, cast, and crew
6. a motion picture technique that creates the illusion of motion rather than recording it with a camera as live action
7. play the part of characters in a movie

actors
animation
art director
cinematographer
costume designer
director
documentaries
Oscar
producer
screenwriter

Political Elections

Across

1. _____ _____ provide secrecy and simplify vote counting.

3. A _____ is a person who is selected by others as a contestant for office.

4. _____ for voting must be approximately equal in population to ensure each vote would have equal power in the election process.

6. _____ is the process by which a person's name is added to the list of qualified voters.

8. _____ is the right to vote.

Down

1. The _____ _____ _____ protects the rights of African Americans and members of other minority groups to vote.

2. _____ is the process by which people vote for the candidate or proposal of their choice.

3. A _____ consists of paid staff members and consultants and unpaid volunteers to help win votes for a certain candidate.

5. Social scientists have found more _____ vote than men.

7. A _____ is the method of secret voting either by voting machines or printed ballots.

ballot
campaign
candidate
districts
election
registration
suffrage
voting machines
Voting Rights Act
women

Solar System

A solar system is made up of a star and the planets or other objects orbiting around it. Our solar system includes Earth and eight other planets that revolve around the sun, which is our star. In our solar system there are many smaller objects such as asteroids, meteoroids, and comets. There is also a thin cloud of dust known as the interplanetary medium. More than 60 moons, also called satellites, orbit the planets. Astronomers have discovered planets orbiting distant stars and hope to learn more about our solar system by studying the masses and orbits of those systems.

Earth
Jupiter
Mars
Mercury
Moon
Neptune
Pluto
Saturn
Sun
Uranus
Venus

Across

2. the only planet whose surface can be seen in detail from Earth
3. a satellite of Earth whose light is reflected light from the sun, as it gives off no light of its own
4. has 15 moons and at least 11 rings around it discovered by photographs taken by the U.S. Voyager 2 space craft
6. the second largest planet, encircled by seven major rings
8. the largest planet in our solar system
9. the most distant planet from the sun
10. the only planet known to support life

Down

1. known as the earth's "twin" because the two planets are so similar in size
2. the nearest planet to the sun
5. a huge, glowing ball of gases at the center of the solar system
7. named for the Roman god of the sea

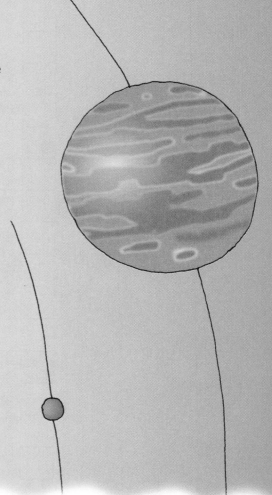

56

Yellowstone National Park

Yellowstone National Park was established in 1872 and is the oldest national park in the world. The park occupies 3,471.51 square miles in the northwestern corner of Wyoming and overlaps into Montana and Idaho. There is no other place of the same size that has as many natural wonders. Geysers, hot springs, sparkling lakes and rivers, and deep canyons attract over a million visitors a year. Yellowstone is the largest wildlife preserve in the United States. A large number of animals, including elk, deer, antelope, mountain sheep, buffalo, moose, and grizzly bears, roam the park freely. The park is famous for some of the best fishing in the West, which is allowed under federal regulations.

Across

1. Volcanoes and _____ shaped the landscape of Yellowstone through millions of years.
4. Yellowstone Lake is the largest _____ _____ lake in North America.
5. Yellowstone Park is located mainly in _____ .
7. Molten rock called _____ lies below the surface of the park and furnishes the heat for the park's geysers and hot springs.
9. In 1872, _____ passed a bill to establish the park and preserve its natural resources.

Down

2. The Yellowstone region was acquired in 1803 as part of the _____ _____ .
3. The park's _____ forests were caused by lava ash during volcanic eruptions over 60,000 years ago.
6. Old Faithful is a famous _____ in the park.
8. The park was named for yellow _____ that lie along part of the Yellowstone River.

Congress   magma
glaciers   petrified
geyser   rocks
high-altitude   Wyoming
Louisiana Purchase

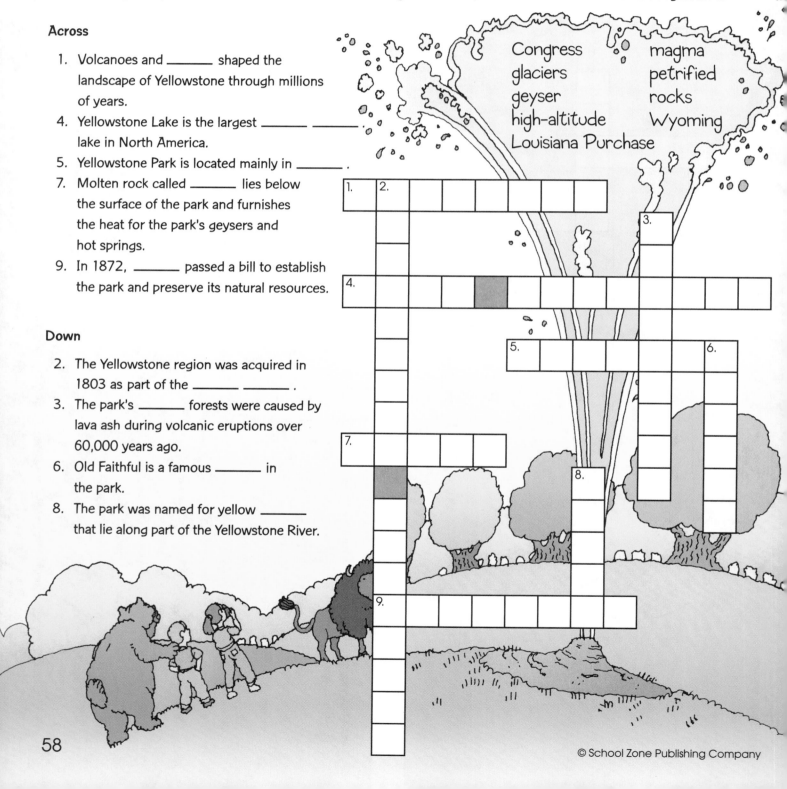

South America

Across

1. Only the Nile River is longer than the _____ River that flows mainly through Brazil.
3. Venezuela is one of the world's leading producers and exporters of _____ , which has made the country one of the wealthiest on the continent.
5. _____ is the largest country in South America in both area and population.
6. The _____ mountains that stretch along Chile's eastern border are the world's longest mountain range above sea level.
8. _____ borders five other countries, the Pacific Ocean, and the Caribbean Sea.

Down

1. _____ _____ in Venezuela has the longest drop of any other waterfall in the world.
2. The _____ is a fertile plain that covers about one fifth of Argentina and has some of the richest topsoil in the world.
4. More than one third of South America is covered by _____ forests.
7. _____ was named for the equator that crosses the country.

Amazon
Andes
Angel Falls
Brazil
Colombia
Ecuador
Pampa
petroleum
rain

Architecture

Architects design more than one kind of structure. Houses, schools, stadiums, and skyscrapers are a few of the many kinds that skilled builders have created throughout history. The Great Pyramid in Egypt was built some 4,500 years ago as a tomb. It was entirely solid, so an immense amount of stone was used to build it. In today's world, advances in engineering eliminate the need for heavy walls. Modern buildings can be much taller than those of the past, built of lightweight outer frameworks of steel and glass. Some of the world's tallest buildings are in cities where people live and work. Architecture is one of the oldest art forms, and many important works of architecture have survived for centuries.

Across

1. a large structure for spectators built around a field
3. a place where people go to be taught
4. the home fortress of a monarch
7. where medical services are provided

Down

1. an exceptionally tall building
2. where a collection of objects is displayed, many from the past
5. a place that provides overnight lodging for the public
6. a single building where people live, some big, some small

castle
hospital
hotel
house
museum
• school
skyscraper
stadium

Rocks

To learn more about the earth's crust, geologists examine various rock samples. By using a microscope, they can study the different minerals that make up a rock's composition. Minerals are made up from atoms and molecules of different degrees of hardness. Diamond, the hardest, can cut glass. The hardness of a mineral is often used to identify it. All minerals came originally from the earth's hot interior, but at the surface they form three kinds of rock: sedimentary, metamorphic, and igneous. Sedimentary rocks are formed in thin layers from materials that were part of older rocks or of plants and animals. Over millions of years, the mass is compressed by the weight of more sand and solidifies into sedimentary rock. Geologists can tell the age of a bed of sedimentary rock by examining the fossils that it contains. Metamorphic rock is made when other rock is altered by extreme heat or pressure. Ninety percent of the earth's crust is made from igneous rock formed from hot magma (molten rock) that wells up from the earth's interior. The materials rocks are made of are continually recycled to make new rocks in a process called the rock cycle.

Across

3. Atoms and molecules make up _____ .
4. The hardest mineral is _____ .
6. Geologists use a _____ to examine rocks.
8. Rocks that are formed in thin layers are _____ rock.

Down

1. Ninety percent of the earth's crust is made from _____ rock.
2. Minerals can be identified by their _____ .
3. Heat and pressure change other rock into _____ rock.
5. The age of sedimentary rock can be determined by _____ found in it.
7. Igneous rock is formed from hot _____ rock.

diamond
fossils
hardness
igneous
magma
metamorphic
microscope
minerals
sedimentary

Made by Nature or People?

Across

2. a public road
7. a landform that is much higher than its surroundings
8. a structure carrying a roadway over water or an obstacle
9. a dock or basin providing mooring for motorboats or yachts
10. a permanent road of rails providing a track for locomotives

Down

1. a large inland body of water
3. a tract of land surrounded by water and smaller than a continent
4. a very steep descent of water from a stream to a lower level
5. a dense growth of trees and underbrush covering a large area
6. a large body of water that flows overland in a long channel

bridge
forest
highway
island
lake
marina
mountain
railroad
river
waterfall

Answer Key

Page 1

Across	Down
3. horse	1. sheep
4. cow	2. chicken
5. pigs	6. goose
7. goat	8. turkey
9. rabbit	

Page 2

Across	Down
4. light	1. rattle
5. file	2. plant
7. pound	3. kind
8. ball	6. hand
	7. play

Page 3

Across	Down
1. pickup	1. platform
2. tank	3. garbage
4. van	6. panel
5. dump	
7. concrete	

Pages 4–5

Across	Down
1. Mouse	2. Spider
4. Jack and Jill	3. Humpty Dumpty
6. Old Woman	4. Jack
7. Peter	5. London
8. Cow	9. Three
10. Little Bo Peep	
11. Mary	

Page 6

Across	Down
5. umbrella	1. kennel
6. postcard	2. souvenir
9. holiday	3. boat
10. pool	4. map
11. car	7. camping
12. airplane	8. vacation
14. tourist	13. hotel
15. suitcase	14. train

Page 7

Across	Down
2. spinnerets	1. silk
6. poison	3. eight
8. insect	4. two
9. bones	5. food
	7. webs

Page 8

Across	Down
1. bee	1. butterfly
4. horse fly	2. mosquito
6. termite	3. firefly
7. mayfly	5. ladybug
8. ant	
9. dragonfly	

Page 9

Across	Down
1. buzz	1. beep
3. jingle	2. hiss
4. pop	5. peep
6. crash	6. click
8. meow	7. tweet

Page 10

Across	Down
1. roots	2. seed
3. wood	4. deciduous
5. evergreen	6. grow
7. food	
8. botanists	
9. soil and water	

Page 11

Across	Down
2. lungs	1. plates
5. temperature	3. backbone
7. dinosaur	4. reptiles
8. land	6. shell

Page 12

Across	Down
4. whisper	1. discuss
5. scream	2. speak
7. joke	3. brag
8. chat	6. report

Page 13

Across	Down
3. kelp forests	1. waves
6. sea horse	2. rockfish
8. roots	3. tidal pools
9. coral reefs	5. polyps
	7. tides

Page 14

Across	Down
5. carbohydrates	1. sugar
6. milk	2. fruits
7. starches	3. meat
8. fat	4. vegetables
9. salt	
10. pasta	

Page 15

Across	Down
3. honeycomb	1. drones
6. flowers	2. worker
8. insects	3. honey
	4. hives
	5. queen's
	7. sting

Pages 16–17

Across	Down
1. giraffe	1. goat
5. bat	2. rabbit
6. elk	3. elephant
7. horse	4. whale
9. cat	8. raccoon
10. zebra	9. cheetah
11. wolf	12. fox
13. hippo	

Page 18

Across	Down
1. cabin	1. cottage
4. apartment	2. walls
7. houseboat	3. castle
8. roof	5. teepee
10. igloo	6. door
	9. floor

Page 19

Across	Down
2. rain forests	1. grasslands
4. salt water	3. desert
8. ocean	5. tundra
10. wetland	6. forest
	7. ponds
	9. swamps

Pages 20–21

Across	Down
2. elephants	1. band
5. acrobats	3. parade
8. trapeze	4. rings
9. horses	6. costumes
10. jugglers	7. clowns
11. roustabouts	8. tigers
13. Big Top	12. tricks

Page 22

Across	Down
3. table tennis	1. volleyball
5. softball	2. basketball
6. bowling	3. tennis
9. football	4. squash
	6. baseball
	7. golf
	8. soccer

Page 23

Across	Down
3. fat	1. walrus
5. polar bear	2. fur
7. skin	4. hoofs
9. rubbery	6. hibernate
10. front	8. zero

Page 24

Across	Down
2. Go	1. Monopoly
3. Trivial Pursuit	4. Checkers
4. Candy Land	6. Scrabble
5. Chess	
7. Chutes & Ladders	
8. Clue	

Page 25

Across	Down
1. snowboarding	1. skateboarding
3. soccer	2. basketball
5. tennis	4. bowling
7. baseball	6. football
9. hockey	8. squash
10. golf	

Page 26

Across	Down
3. avalanche	1. cyclones
5. tornado	2. blizzard
7. earthquake	4. flood
8. hurricane	5. tsunami
	6. typhoons

Page 27

Across	Down
2. salt	1. water
3. steer	3. surface
5. mammals	4. walrus
7. blowhole	6. blue
8. seals	

Pages 28–29

Across	Down
3. Gutenberg	1. Wright
5. Lister	2. Benz and Daimler
6. Edison	3. Graham Bell
7. Kellogg	4. Franklin

Pages 30–31

Across	Down
4. February	1. May
6. July	2. September
7. November	3. January
8. December	5. October

Page 32

Across	Down
4. oil	1. frogs
5. hummingbirds	2. down
8. toes	3. straight
	6. molt
	7. cones

Page 33

Across	Down
4. Lake Michigan	1. Pacific
6. fifty	2. Alaska
7. Wyoming	3. Mississippi
8. California	5. New York
10. Rhode Island	9. Atlantic

Answer Key

Page 34

Across
1. players
7. racket
9. love
10. doubles
11. set
12. net

Down
1. point
2. ace
3. singles
4. deuce
5. service
6. ball
8. court

Page 35

Across
b. quotient
d. fraction
g. denominator
h. divisor
i. product
j. sets
k. factors

Down
a. sum
c. numerator
e. remainder
f. difference
g. dividend

Pages 36–37

Across
2. Greyhound
6. Retriever
7. Setter
8. Afghan
10. Boxer
11. Dalmation

Down
1. Husky
2. Great Dane
3. Dachshund
4. Pointer
5. Beagle
9. Poodle

Pages 38–39

Across
2. subway
4. taxicab
5. motorcycle
7. bicycle
8. truck

Down
1. automobile
2. streetcar
3. bus
6. train

Page 40

Across
1. passengers
3. control tower
6. tickets
7. hangars
8. gate
10. baggage

Down
1. pilot
2. security guards
4. runways
5. terminal
9. fuel

Page 41

Across
5. square
6. rectangle
7. cone
8. cylinder

Down
1. circle
2. sphere
3. triangle
4. cube

Page 42

Across
1. mosquito
3. cockroach
5. vampire
6. fleas
9. gypsy moth

Down
2. scorpion
4. housefly
7. termites
8. rat

Page 43

Across
1. temperature
3. weather
7. precipitation
8. condensation

Down
2. evaporation
4. air pressure
5. water
6. wind

Page 44

Across
1. grow
2. mammals
4. capybaras
5. diseases
6. rodents
8. herbivorous

Down
1. gnawing
2. mice
3. scientists
7. fur

Page 45

Across
2. pitcher
6. diamond
7. bat
8. five
9. umpire
11. base
13. outfield
14. glove

Down
1. strike
3. home
4. run
5. catcher
8. fly ball
10. inning
12. Series
13. outs

Page 46

Across
2. carnivore
4. water cycle
6. habitat
7. ecology
8. herbivore
9. omnivores
10. botany

Down
1. parasite
3. meteorology
5. oxygen

Page 47

Across
1. eyes
2. muscles
4. heart
5. lungs
7. brain

Down
1. ears
3. skeleton
6. skin
7. blood

Pages 48–49

Across
2. printing press
3. television
4. satellite
5. computer
6. map
7. wheel
8. camera
9. airplane

Down
1. microscope
2. plow
3. telephone
5. clock

Page 50

Across
1. sunspots
5. galaxy
6. life
7. light & heat
10. yellow dwarf

Down
1. solar flares
2. star
3. gas
4. Milky Way
8. energy
9. core

Page 51

Across
2. pronouns
5. nouns
6. interjections
7. adverbs

Down
1. conjunctions
2. prepositions
3. adjectives
4. verbs

Pages 52–53

Across
1. Wilson
4. Kennedy
5. G.W. Bush
7. Lincoln
8. T. Roosevelt
9. Reagan
10. Ford
11. Nixon

Down
1. Washington
2. F.D. Roosevelt
3. Jefferson
6. Clinton
8. Truman

Page 54

Across
1. cinematographer
2. screenwriter
3. producer
5. documentaries
8. art director
9. Oscar

Down
1. costume designer
4. director
6. animation
7. actors

Page 55

Across
1. voting machines
3. candidate
4. districts
6. registration
8. suffrage

Down
1. Voting Rights Act
2. election
3. campaign
5. women
7. ballot

Pages 56–57

Across
2. Mars
3. Moon
4. Uranus
6. Saturn
8. Jupiter
9. Pluto
10. Earth

Down
1. Venus
2. Mercury
5. Sun
7. Neptune

Page 58

Across
1. glaciers
4. high-altitude
5. Wyoming
7. magma
9. Congress

Down
2. Louisiana Purchase
3. petrified
6. geyser
8. rocks

Page 59

Across
1. Amazon
3. petroleum
5. Brazil
6. Andes
8. Colombia

Down
1. Angel Falls
2. Pampa
4. rain
7. Ecuador

Page 60

Across
1. stadium
3. school
4. castle
7. hospital

Down
1. skyscraper
2. museum
5. hotel
6. house

Page 61

Across
3. minerals
4. diamond
6. microscope
8. sedimentary

Down
1. igneous
2. hardness
3. metamorphic
5. fossils
7. magma

Page 62

Across
2. highway
7. mountain
8. bridge
9. marina
10. railroad

Down
1. lake
3. island
4. waterfall
5. forest
6. river

   Crosswords, Ages 8-Up **02352**